Peripheral neuropathy diet cookbook

Healthy and Delicious Nerve-Friendly Recipes to Prevent and Manage Neuropathy Symptoms

David T. Salcedo

HOW TO USE THIS COOKBOOK

Acquaint yourself with the content: Begin by reading the cookbook's parts, which contain useful information about peripheral neuropathy, dietary considerations, and the role of nutrition in symptom management.

Explore the Recipes: Spend some time browsing the cookbook's broad variety of recipes. Whether you're looking for breakfast ideas, lunch options, dinner dishes, snacks, or smoothies, there's something for every meal and occasion. Pay Attention to Nutritional Information: Each dish provides complete nutritional information per serving, allowing you to make more educated decisions regarding your diet. Consider the following factors: calories, protein, fat, carbs, fiber, and sugar content.

Consider Your Preferences and Dietary Needs: Select recipes that are compatible with your taste preferences, dietary limitations, and nutritional needs. With so many alternatives accessible, you can find recipes that meet your specific needs and interests.

Plan Your Meals: Incorporate the recipes into your weekly meal plan to guarantee a well-balanced and diverse diet.

Prepare ahead of time by choosing dishes for the week, creating a shopping list, and stockpiling the essential ingredients.

Prepare Ingredients and Cooking Equipment: Before you start cooking, gather all of the ingredients and cooking equipment required for the meal. Make sure your kitchen is well-stocked with key tools including pots, pans, knives, and measuring spoons.

Follow the directions: Carefully adhere to the step-by-step directions provided for each recipe. To get the finest results, pay close attention to ingredient quantities, cooking times, and cooking styles.

Experiment & Customize: Feel free to experiment with ingredient substitutions or modify recipes to suit your tastes. Don't be scared to get creative and invent your own recipes.

Enjoy Your Meals: Once the cooking is finished, sit down and enjoy the tasty and nutritious meals you've made. Enjoy the flavors, textures, and nourishment that each recipe offers.

INTRODUCTION

Alex, a passionate architect recognized for his originality and dedication to his work, lived in the city's bustling center, nestled among the vivid streets. Alex's confident exterior concealed a secret struggle: peripheral neuropathy.

It began with tingling sensations and numbness in his feet and progressively spread up his legs. At first, Alex disregarded it as weariness from working long hours on construction sites. However, as the symptoms persisted and worsened, he realized he could no longer ignore them.

After talking with his doctor, Alex discovered that his peripheral neuropathy was most likely caused by his uncontrolled diabetes. Faced with the scary prospect of lifetime medicine and probable problems, Alex decided to take charge of his health in a new way: through his nutrition.

Alex set out on a dietary transformation adventure, armed with drive and a renewed sense of purpose. He became engrossed in study, reading information on foods that could potentially relieve neuropathic symptoms and balance blood sugar.

Gone were the days of easy foods and sugary treats. Instead, Alex stocked his kitchen with nutritious items like colorful fruits and vegetables, lean proteins, and entire grains. He experimented with dishes that emphasized elements known to nourish the nerves, such as vitamin B12-rich fish and antioxidant-rich leafy greens.

Every meal provided Alex with an opportunity to replenish his body while also soothing his ruffled nerves. He savored each piece attentively, enjoying the flavors as well as the awareness that he was taking proactive actions to improve his health.

As the weeks passed into months, Alex noticed tiny changes. The tingling sensations in his feet faded, replaced by a renewed sense of vitality. His energy levels skyrocketed, allowing him to approach his work with newfound zeal and intensity.

Encouraged by his progress, Alex added regular exercise to his routine, which increased the effects of his nutritional changes. He took daily walks around the city streets, relishing the sensation of his feet connecting with the pavement beneath him—a simple pleasure he had previously taken for granted.

Alex's peripheral neuropathy gradually improved, demonstrating the transforming impact of nutrition and lifestyle changes. Encouraged by his accomplishment, he became an advocate for others with similar issues, sharing his experience and providing advice on how to regain control of their health.

Despite his difficult path, Alex emerged stronger and more resilient than ever before. Through devotion, perseverance, and a nutritious diet, he not only treated his peripheral neuropathy, but also experienced a renewed sense of empowerment—a reminder that sometimes the most significant transformations begin with a single, intentional choice.

WHAT IS PERIPHERAL NEUROPATHY

Peripheral neuropathy is a condition that damages the peripheral nerves, which are located outside of the brain and spinal cord. These nerves convey messages between the body and the central nervous system, controlling movements, sensations, and organ function.

Causes

1. Diabetes is one of the most common causes of peripheral neuropathy, specifically diabetic neuropathy.

2. Trauma or Injury: Physical injury, such as an accident or repetitive stress, can cause nerve damage.

3. Autoimmune Diseases: Conditions such as rheumatoid arthritis, lupus, and Guillain-Barré syndrome can cause nerve injury.

4. Certain diseases, such as HIV/AIDS, Lyme disease, and shingles, can result in neuropathy.

5. Toxins: Heavy metals, chemotherapeutic treatments, and some pharmaceuticals can all cause nerve injury.

6. Genetics: Some people may inherit conditions that predispose them to peripheral neuropathy.

Symptoms

1.Tingling or numbness: Typically in the hands, feet, or both.

2.Burning or sharp pain is a typical symptom that can be persistent or intermittent.

3.Muscle weakness: Difficulty in fine motor skills and coordination.

4.Touch Sensitivity: Even a mild touch might be uncomfortable.

5.Reflexes are diminished, notably in the ankles.

6.Sensation changes include feeling as if you're wearing gloves or socks when you aren't or walking on cushions.

Treatment

1.Pain medications, such as over-the-counter painkillers or prescription pharmaceuticals like gabapentin and pregabalin, may be administered to treat pain.

2.Physical therapy: Exercises that enhance strength, flexibility, and balance can help control symptoms and avoid complications.

3.Transcutaneous Electrical Nerve Stimulation (TENS): A device that sends tiny electrical impulses to damaged nerves, which can help alleviate pain.

4.Lifestyle Changes: Managing underlying illnesses such as diabetes, quitting smoking, and limiting alcohol use might help reduce the course of neuropathy.

5.Alternative Therapies: Acupuncture, massage therapy, and biofeedback may help some people.

Risk Factors

1.Diabetes: Particularly poorly managed diabetes.

2.Risk increases with age, as nerve health naturally deteriorates.

3.Toxins include heavy metals, certain drugs, and chemicals.

4.Family History: Genetics may be a factor in predisposing some people to neuropathy.

5.Certain Medical Conditions: Kidney illness, liver disease, and autoimmune disorders all raise the risk.

6.Alcoholism: Excessive alcohol use can cause nerve damage.

Preventive Measures

1.Manage Underlying Conditions: Keep diabetes, autoimmune illnesses, and infections under control.

2.Healthy Lifestyle Choices: Eat a balanced diet, exercise regularly, avoid smoking, and use alcohol in moderation.

3.Avoid Toxins: Limit your exposure to toxins and chemicals that can harm your nerves.

4.Regular check-ups: Schedule regular visits to healthcare providers for screenings and early detection of potential concerns.

5. Proper Ergonomics: If your profession requires repeated movements or lengthy periods of sitting or standing, take breaks and use correct ergonomics to lessen the chance of nerve injury.

IMPORTANCE OF DIET FOR MANAGING PERIPHERAL NEUROPATHY

Nutrition is crucial for sustaining healthy nerve health. The nervous system requires a wide range of nutrients to function effectively, from supporting nerve cell structure and function to promoting neurotransmitter generation and signal transmission. Here's a thorough examination of how eating influences nerve health:

1. Structured Support

Omega-3 and omega-6 fatty acids are essential for maintaining healthy nerve cell membranes. They contribute to the integrity and fluidity of cell membranes, allowing for effective signal transmission.

Phospholipids: Phospholipids, including phosphatidylcholine and phosphatidylserine, are necessary components of nerve cell membranes. They help to maintain membrane integrity and promote cell-to-cell communication.

Proteins: Dietary proteins contain amino acids, which are used to construct nerve cells. They are needed for the production of neurotransmitters, enzymes, and structural proteins required for nerve function and repair.

2. Neurotransmitter Production

Amino Acids: Tryptophan, tyrosine, and phenylalanine are precursors of neurotransmitters such as serotonin, dopamine, and norepinephrine. Adequate intake of these amino acids is critical for maintaining normal neurotransmitter levels, which are required for mood control, cognition, and motor performance.

Several vitamins and minerals play important roles in neurotransmitter production and function. For example, vitamin B6 is required for the conversion of tryptophan to serotonin, and iron and zinc are necessary cofactors for dopamine production.

3.Antioxidant Protection

Vitamins C and E: These antioxidants help nerve cells resist oxidative damage caused by free radicals. Oxidative stress can cause nerve cell damage and neuropathic symptoms.

Selenium and zinc are essential components of antioxidant enzymes, which neutralize free radicals and protect nerve cells from oxidative damage.

Polyphenols, which can be found in fruits, vegetables, and plant-based diets, contain antioxidant and anti-inflammatory qualities that help to maintain nerve function and protect against neurodegenerative disease.

4. Blood Sugar Regulation

Complex carbs: Fiber-rich, complex carbs digest more slowly, resulting in steady blood sugar increases and avoiding dramatic spikes and crashes. Stable blood sugar levels are crucial for avoiding nerve damage and diabetic neuropathy.

Healthy Fats: Eating healthy fats such nuts, seeds, avocados, and fatty fish can help increase insulin sensitivity and lower the risk of insulin resistance, which is a precursor to diabetes-related neuropathy.

5. Inflammation reduction

Omega-3 Fatty Acids: EPA (eicosapentaenoic acid) and DHA (docosahexaenoic acid), found in fatty fish such as salmon and mackerel, have anti-inflammatory qualities that can help reduce inflammation in nerve tissues and alleviate neuropathic pain.

Curcumin: Curcumin, the main ingredient in turmeric, has significant anti-inflammatory properties that may help relieve nerve pain and inflammation caused by neuropathy.

6. Micronutrient Support

Deficiency in vitamin B12 can cause nerve damage and neuropathic symptoms. Adequate diet of vitamin B12-rich foods, such as meat, fish, dairy products, and fortified cereals, is required to maintain nerve health.

Magnesium has an important role in nerve function and muscle contraction. Low magnesium levels have been linked to neuropathic symptoms, thus consuming magnesium-rich foods such as leafy greens, nuts, seeds, and whole grains is essential for nerve function.

Key Nutrients for Nerve Function

Key nutrients are essential for nerve function, since they aid in maintaining the structure, integrity, and communication of nerve cells throughout the body. Here's a comprehensive breakdown of the major nutrients required for nerve health.

1. Vitamin B 12

Vitamin B12 is required for the formation of myelin, a protective coating of nerve fibers that aids in nerve signal transmission. Vitamin B12 deficiency can cause nerve damage and neurological symptoms include tingling, numbness, and muscular weakness. Foods high in vitamin B12 include meat, fish, dairy products, eggs, and fortified cereals.

2. Omega 3 Fatty Acids

EPA (eicosapentaenoic acid) and DHA (docosahexaenoic acid), two omega-3 fatty acids found in fatty fish such as salmon, mackerel, and sardines, are essential for nerve cell membrane formation and function. They contribute to nerve signal transmission, reduce inflammation in nerve tissues, and enhance general nerve health.

3. Vitamin B6

Vitamin B6, commonly known as pyridoxine, aids in the manufacture of neurotransmitters like serotonin, dopamine, and gamma-aminobutyric acid (GABA). These neurotransmitters have important roles in mood regulation, cognitive function, and motor control. Vitamin B6 deficiency can cause neuropathy and other neurological problems. Chicken, salmon, bananas, potatoes, and chickpeas are good sources of vitamin B6.

4. Vitamin E

Vitamin E is a powerful antioxidant that protects nerve cells from oxidative damage produced by free radicals. It promotes nerve health by protecting cell membranes and lowering inflammation. Nuts, seeds, vegetable oils, and leafy green vegetables are rich in vitamin E.

5. Magnesium

Magnesium is involved in many metabolic events in the body, such as nerve signal transmission and muscle contraction. It serves as a cofactor for enzymes involved in nerve function and neurotransmitter release. Low magnesium levels can cause nerve hyperexcitability and raise the risk of neuropathic complaints. Magnesium-rich foods include leafy greens, nuts, seeds, whole grains, and legumes.

6. Antioxidants

Antioxidants including vitamin C, E, selenium, and zinc protect nerve cells from oxidative stress and damage. They neutralize free radicals, which are extremely reactive chemicals that can damage cells and lead to nerve degeneration. A diet rich in fruits, vegetables, nuts, seeds, and whole grains contains a range of antioxidants that promote nerve health.

7. Alpha Lipoic Acid

Alpha-lipoic acid is a potent antioxidant that promotes the regeneration of other antioxidants including vitamin C and vitamin E. It has been proven to increase nerve function, decrease neuropathic pain, and treat diabetic neuropathy symptoms. Alpha-lipoic acid is present in trace levels in foods such as spinach, broccoli, potatoes, and organ meats, but it is also accessible as a nutritional supplement.

8. Zinc

Zinc is essential for nervous system signaling, neurotransmitter production, and DNA repair. It affects the action of enzymes that control nerve cell growth and repair. Zinc deficiency can affect nerve function and cause neuropathic symptoms. Oysters, meat, chicken, nuts, seeds, and whole grains are all good sources of zinc.

IMPORTANCE OF ESSENTIAL NUTRIENTS FOR NERVE HEALTH

Understanding Vitamin B12

Importance for nerve function

Vitamin B12 (cobalamin) is a water-soluble vitamin that is essential for nerve function and overall neurological health. It is necessary for the production of myelin, the protective sheath that surrounds nerve fibers and allows for efficient nerve signal transmission. Nerve cells can be destroyed if vitamin B12 levels are low, resulting in neurological symptoms as tingling, numbness, and weakness.

Vitamin B12 is important in the creation of neurotransmitters, which are molecules that send impulses between nerve cells. It specifically helps to synthesize serotonin, dopamine, and norepinephrine, all of which are important for mood control, cognition, and motor function. Furthermore, vitamin B12 is required for the survival of healthy nerve cells and the repair of damaged nerves.

Vitamin B12 deficiency can cause peripheral neuropathy, which is defined as nerve damage in the peripheral nervous system. Symptoms of peripheral neuropathy include numbness or tingling in the hands and feet, trouble walking, muscle weakness, and balance issues. In severe situations, vitamin B12 deficiency can cause permanent nerve damage and neurological issues.

Dietary sources and supplements

Vitamin B12 is largely found in animal-derived foods, making it difficult for vegans and vegetarians to receive enough through diet alone. Some of the finest dietary sources of vitamin B12 are:

- Meats including beef, hog, lamb, and chicken provide high levels of vitamin B12.
- Fatty fish, like salmon, trout, tuna, and mackerel, contain significant levels of vitamin B12.
- Shellfish such as clams, oysters, mussels, and crab contain high levels of vitamin B12.
- Dairy products such as milk, cheese, yogurt, and eggs include vitamin B12, which is especially beneficial for lacto-ovo vegetarians.

Supplementation may be required for people who are unable to receive enough vitamin B12 from their diet. Vitamin B12 supplements come in a variety of formats, including oral tablets, sublingual tablets, and injections. Individuals with digestive disorders that limit vitamin B12 absorption may benefit more from sublingual tablets, which are dissolved beneath the tongue.

Omega-3 fatty acids and anti-inflammatory foods

Benefits of Nerve Health

Omega-3 fatty acids are necessary polyunsaturated fats that help to keep nerves healthy and functional. These fatty acids, notably eicosapentaenoic acid (EPA) and docosahexaenoic acid (DHA), have been demonstrated to have anti-inflammatory characteristics, which may help reduce inflammation in nerve tissues and improve neuropathy symptoms. Here are some major advantages of omega-3 fatty acids for nerve health:

- Reduced Inflammation: Chronic inflammation is a common cause of many neurological illnesses, including peripheral neuropathy. Omega-3 fatty acids aid to reduce inflammation by decreasing the synthesis of pro-inflammatory cytokines and lowering the expression of inflammatory genes in nerve cells.

- Enhanced Nerve Cell Function: Omega-3 fatty acids are essential components of nerve cell membranes, where they contribute to membrane fluidity and integrity. This is required for proper nerve signal transmission and communication among nerve cells.

- Omega-3 fatty acids are antioxidants that help neutralize free radicals and protect nerve cells from oxidative damage. This is especially critical for those with neuropathy, as oxidative stress can worsen nerve damage and increase symptom severity.

- Improved Blood Flow: Omega-3 fatty acids have been proven to increase blood flow to peripheral nerves, potentially improving nutrition delivery and oxygenation of nerve tissues. This may aid in nerve healing and regeneration in people with neuropathic disorders.

Antioxidants and phytonutrients

Fighting Oxidative Stress and Inflammation

Antioxidants and phytonutrients are potent molecules present in plant-based diets that play critical roles in fighting oxidative stress and inflammation in the body. Oxidative stress occurs when the body's free radicals and antioxidants are out of balance, causing cell, tissue, and organ damage. Chronic inflammation, which is caused by a variety of reasons including poor diet, stress, and environmental contaminants, can also contribute to the development of chronic diseases such as heart disease, diabetes, and cancer.

Antioxidants operate by neutralizing free radicals, which are unstable chemicals that can cause cell damage and contribute to oxidative stress. Phytonutrients, also known as phytochemicals, are plant-derived bioactive substances with antioxidant and anti-inflammatory activities. Antioxidants and phytonutrients work together to protect cells from harm, reduce inflammation, and improve general health.

FOODS TO INCLUDE AND FOOD TO AVOID

Peripheral neuropathy patients can benefit from a well-planned diet that includes foods high in nutrients required for nerve health while avoiding those that may aggravate symptoms or contribute to nerve damage. Here's a comprehensive list of foods to include and avoid for people with peripheral neuropathy:

Foods To Include

1.Omega-3 Fatty Acids: Fatty fish such as salmon, mackerel, and sardines are high in omega-3 fatty acids, which are anti-inflammatory and help nerve cells operate.

2.Leafy Green Vegetables: Spinach, kale, and other leafy greens are high in vitamins, minerals, and antioxidants, which improve nerve function and protect against oxidative stress.

3.Berries: Blueberries, strawberries, and raspberries are high in antioxidants, vitamins, and phytonutrients, which assist in reducing inflammation and improve neurological function.

4.Nuts and Seeds: Almonds, walnuts, flaxseeds, and chia seeds are abundant in vitamin E, magnesium, and omega-3 fatty acids, which are beneficial to nerve function.

5.Lean Proteins: Skinless poultry, lean cuts of beef, pig, and tofu include critical amino acids for nerve cell repair and neurotransmitter production.

6.Whole Grains: Quinoa, brown rice, oats, and whole wheat products are high in B vitamins, magnesium, and fiber, which help nerve function and manage blood sugar.

7.Avocados are high in healthy fats, particularly monounsaturated fats, which promote nerve cell membrane integrity and prevent inflammation.

8.Legumes: Beans, lentils, and chickpeas are high in protein, fiber, and vital elements including magnesium and B vitamins.

9.Colorful bell peppers contain vitamin C, an antioxidant that protects nerve cells from oxidative damage.

10.Turmeric's main ingredient, curcumin, has anti-inflammatory and antioxidant effects that may help treat neuropathic pain and inflammation.

Foods To Avoid

1.Processed meals, such as fast food, packaged snacks, and sugary sweets, are high in unhealthy fats, refined sugars, and additives, all of which can worsen inflammation and cause nerve damage.

2.Sugary Foods and Beverages: Refined sugar-rich foods such as soda, candy, and pastries can induce blood sugar increases and exacerbate diabetic neuropathy symptoms.

3.Trans fats, which are present in fried foods, margarine, and processed snacks, can cause inflammation and oxidative stress, compromising nerve health.

4.Excessive alcohol consumption can decrease nerve function and worsen neuropathy symptoms, particularly in people who have alcohol-related neuropathy.

5.High-Sodium Foods: Consuming too much sodium can cause fluid retention and raise blood pressure, thereby exacerbating neuropathy and other cardiovascular issues.

6.Artificial Sweeteners: Some artificial sweeteners have neurotoxic properties and can impair nerve function in sensitive people.

7.Refined carbohydrates, such as white bread and rice, can induce fast rises and dips in blood sugar levels, exacerbating diabetic neuropathy symptoms.

8.Fried and fatty foods: Foods heavy in harmful fats, such as deep-fried foods, processed meats, and fatty cuts of meat, can cause inflammation and nerve damage.

9.Caffeine: While moderate caffeine use is normally safe, it might disturb sleep patterns and worsen neuropathy symptoms in some people.

10.High-Glycemic Foods: High-glycemic index foods, such as white bread, sugary cereals, and potatoes, can produce rapid blood sugar spikes and worsen diabetic neuropathy symptoms.

NOTE

CHAPTER 1

Breakfast Recipes

1: Berry Chia Seed Pudding

Health Benefits

- Berries are rich in antioxidants and anti-inflammatory compounds, which can help reduce oxidative stress and inflammation associated with peripheral neuropathy.

- Chia seeds are an excellent source of omega-3 fatty acids, which support nerve health and reduce neuropathic pain.

Ingredients

- 1/4 cup chia seeds

- Almond milk of 1 Cup (or any milk of your choice)

- 1/2 teaspoon vanilla extract

- 1 tablespoon maple syrup (optional)

- 1/2 cup mixed berries (such as strawberries, blueberries, and raspberries)

Mode of Preparation

1. In a bowl, mix together chia seeds, almond milk, vanilla extract, and maple syrup (if using). Stir well to combine.

2. Cover the bowl and refrigerate for at least 4 hours or overnight, until the mixture thickens into a pudding-like consistency.

3. Before serving, layer the chia seed pudding with mixed berries in a serving glass or bowl.

4. Optionally, garnish with additional berries or a drizzle of honey before serving.

Nutritional Information (per serving)

- Calories: 180 kcal

- Protein: 5g

- Fat: 8g

- Carbohydrates: 22g

- Fiber: 10g

- Sugar: 8g

Serving Size: 1 serving

Preparation Time: 5 minutes

Cooking Time: 4 hours (chilling time)

2: Avocado Toast with Smoked Salmon

Health Benefits

- Avocado is rich in healthy fats, fiber, and vitamin E, which support nerve function and reduce inflammation.

- Smoked salmon is a good source of omega-3 fatty acids, which can help alleviate neuropathic pain and improve nerve health.

Ingredients

- 1 ripe avocado

- 2 slices of whole-grain bread

- 2 ounces smoked salmon

- 1 tablespoon lemon juice

- Salt and pepper to taste

- Optional toppings: sliced tomatoes, microgreens, or red onion

Mode of Preparation

1. Slices of whole-grain bread should be toasted until golden brown.

2. Mash the ripe avocado in a bowl and mix in lemon juice, salt, and pepper.

3. Mashed avocado should be spread evenly onto the toasted bread slices.

4. Top each slice with smoked salmon and any desired toppings.

5. Serve immediately.

Nutritional Information (per serving)

- Calories: 320 kcal

- Protein: 20g

- Fat: 15g

- Carbohydrates: 25g

- Fiber: 10g

- Sugar: 2g

Serving Size: 1 serving

Preparation Time: 10 minutes

Cooking Time: 5 minutes

3: Spinach and Mushroom Omelette

Health Benefits

- Spinach is rich in vitamin B6 and folate, which support nerve health and reduce neuropathic symptoms.

- Mushrooms contain antioxidants and anti-inflammatory compounds that can help alleviate nerve pain and inflammation.

Ingredients

- 2 large eggs

- 1/2 cup fresh spinach, chopped

- 1/4 cup sliced mushrooms

- 1 tablespoon olive oil

- Salt and pepper to taste

- Optional toppings: shredded cheese, diced tomatoes, or avocado

Mode of Preparation

1. Olive oil should be heated in a non-stick skillet over medium heat.

2. Add sliced mushrooms to the skillet and sauté until golden brown.

3. Beat the eggs in a bowl and season with salt and pepper.

4. Pour the beaten eggs into the skillet, swirling to cover the bottom evenly.

5. Once the edges start to set, add chopped spinach on one half of the omelette.

6. Fold the other half of the omelette over the spinach and mushrooms.

7. Cook for another 1-2 minutes until the omelette is cooked through.

8. Slide the omelette onto a plate and serve hot with optional toppings.

Nutritional Information (per serving)

- Calories: 220 kcal

- Protein: 14g

- Fat: 16g

- Carbohydrates: 4g

- Fiber: 1g

- Sugar: 1g

Serving Size: 1 serving

Preparation Time: 10 minutes

Cooking Time: 5 minutes

4: Quinoa Breakfast Bowl with Almond Butter and Banana

Health Benefits

- Quinoa is a good source of protein, fiber, and magnesium, which support nerve health and reduce neuropathic symptoms.

- Almond butter provides healthy fats and vitamin E, which protect nerve cells from oxidative damage and inflammation.

- Bananas are rich in vitamin B6 and potassium, which support nerve function and help regulate blood pressure.

Ingredients

- 1/2 cup cooked quinoa

- 2 tablespoons almond butter

- 1 ripe banana, sliced

- Honey or maple syrup of 1 tablespoon (optional)

- Optional toppings: chopped nuts, hemp seeds, or dried fruit

Mode of Preparation

1. Cook quinoa according to package instructions and let cool slightly.

2. In a serving bowl, layer cooked quinoa with sliced banana.

3. Drizzle almond butter and honey or maple syrup (if using) over the quinoa and banana.

4. Garnish with optional toppings such as chopped nuts, hemp seeds, or dried fruit.

5. Serve warm and enjoy.

Nutritional Information (per serving)

- Calories: 380 kcal

- Protein: 9g

- Fat: 16g

- Carbohydrates: 54g

- Fiber: 7g

- Sugar: 20g

Serving Size: 1 serving

Preparation Time: 15 minutes

Cooking Time: 15 minutes (for quinoa)

5: Greek Yogurt Parfait with Mixed Berries and Walnuts

Health Benefits

- Greek yogurt is high in protein and probiotics, which support digestive health and may help alleviate neuropathic symptoms.

- Mixed berries are rich in antioxidants and anti-inflammatory compounds that promote nerve health and reduce oxidative stress.

- Walnuts provide omega-3 fatty acids and vitamin E, which protect nerve cells from damage and inflammation.

Ingredients

- 1 cup Greek yogurt (unsweetened)

- 1/2 cup mixed berries (such as strawberries, blueberries, and raspberries)

- 1/4 cup chopped walnuts

- Honey or maple syrup of 1 tablespoon (optional)

- Optional toppings: granola, coconut flakes, or cinnamon

Mode of Preparation

1. In a serving glass or bowl, layer Greek yogurt with mixed berries and chopped walnuts.

2. Drizzle honey or maple syrup (if using) over the yogurt and berries.

3. Garnish with optional toppings such as granola, coconut flakes, or a sprinkle of cinnamon.

4. Serve chilled and enjoy as a nutritious breakfast or snack.

Nutritional Information (per serving)

- Calories: 320 kcal

- Protein: 18g

- Fat: 15g

- Carbohydrates: 30g

- Fiber: 5g

- Sugar: 20g

Serving Size: 1 serving

Preparation Time: 5 minutes

6: Oatmeal with Almond Butter and Berries

Health Benefits

- Oats are a good source of fiber and magnesium, which help regulate blood sugar levels and support nerve health.

- Almond butter provides healthy fats, protein, and vitamin E, which protect nerve cells from oxidative damage.

- Berries are rich in antioxidants and anti-inflammatory compounds that promote nerve health and reduce inflammation.

Ingredients

- 1/2 cup rolled oats

- Water or milk of 1 cup of your choice

- 1 tablespoon almond butter

- 1/4 cup mixed berries (such as strawberries, blueberries, and raspberries)

- Sliced bananas, chopped nuts, or a drizzle of honey but they are optional

Mode of Preparation

1. In a small saucepan, bring water or milk to a boil.

2. Stir in rolled oats and reduce heat to low. Simmer for 5-7 minutes, stirring occasionally, until oats are cooked and thickened.

3. Transfer cooked oats to a serving bowl and swirl in almond butter until evenly distributed.

4. Top with mixed berries and any desired toppings.

5. Serve hot and enjoy as a comforting breakfast.

Nutritional Information (per serving)

- Calories: 300 kcal

- Protein: 9g

- Fat: 12g

- Carbohydrates: 40g

- Fiber: 7g

- Sugar: 5g

Serving Size: 1 serving

Preparation Time: 5 minutes

Cooking Time: 10 minutes

7: Spinach and Feta Egg Muffins

Health Benefits

- Eggs are a good source of protein and vitamin B12, which support nerve health and reduce neuropathic symptoms.

- Spinach is rich in vitamin B6, folate, and antioxidants, which protect nerve cells from damage and inflammation.

- Feta cheese adds flavor and provides calcium, which is important for nerve function and bone health.

Ingredients

- 6 large eggs

- 1 cup fresh spinach, chopped

- 1/4 cup crumbled feta cheese

- Salt and pepper to taste

- Optional add-ins: diced tomatoes, chopped bell peppers, or cooked mushrooms

Mode of Preparation

1. Oven should be pre heated to 350°F (175°C) and grease a muffin tin with cooking spray.

2. In a large mixing bowl, beat the eggs and season with salt and pepper.

3. Stir in chopped spinach, crumbled feta cheese, and any desired add-ins.

4. Pour the egg mixture evenly into the muffin tin, filling each cup about 3/4 full.

5. Bake in the preheated oven for 20-25 minutes, or until the egg muffins are set and lightly golden on top.

6. Remove from the oven and let cool slightly before serving.

Nutritional Information (per serving, 2 muffins):

- Calories: 180 kcal

- Protein: 15g

- Fat: 12g

- Carbohydrates: 3g

- Fiber: 1g

- Sugar: 1g

Serving Size: 1 serving (2 muffins)

Preparation Time: 10 minutes

Cooking Time: 20-25 minutes

8: Blueberry Banana Smoothie Bowl

Health Benefits

- Blueberries are rich in antioxidants called anthocyanins, which have anti-inflammatory properties and support nerve health.

- Bananas provide potassium and vitamin B6, which help regulate nerve function and reduce neuropathic symptoms.

- Greek yogurt adds protein and probiotics, which support digestive health and may alleviate neuropathic symptoms.

Ingredients

- 1 ripe banana, frozen

- 1/2 cup frozen blueberries

- 1/2 cup Greek yogurt (unsweetened)

- Almond milk of 1/4 cup (or any milk of your choice)

- Optional toppings: sliced bananas, fresh blueberries, granola, or shredded coconut

Mode of Preparation

1. In a blender, combine frozen banana, frozen blueberries, Greek yogurt, and almond milk.

2. Blend until smooth and creamy, adding more almond milk if needed to reach desired consistency.

3. Pour the smoothie into a bowl and top with sliced bananas, fresh blueberries, granola, or shredded coconut.

4. Serve immediately and enjoy with a spoon.

Nutritional Information (per serving)

- Calories: 250 kcal

- Protein: 12g

- Fat: 3g

- Carbohydrates: 50g

- Fiber: 8g

- Sugar: 27g

Serving Size: 1 serving

Preparation Time: 5 minutes

9: Sweet Potato Breakfast Hash

Health Benefits

- Sweet potatoes are rich in vitamin B6, potassium, and antioxidants, which support nerve health and reduce inflammation.

- Eggs provide protein and vitamin B12, which are essential for nerve function and repair.

- Spinach adds folate and iron, which help prevent nerve damage and support red blood cell production.

Ingredients

- 1 medium sweet potato, diced

- 2 large eggs

- 1 cup fresh spinach, chopped

- 1/4 cup diced onion

- 1/4 cup diced bell peppers

- 1 tablespoon olive oil

- Salt and pepper to taste

- Optional toppings: avocado slices, salsa, or hot sauce

Mode of Preparation

1. Olive oil should be heated in a skillet over medium heat.

2. Add diced sweet potatoes to the skillet and cook until tender and lightly browned, about 8-10 minutes.

3. Stir in diced onion and bell peppers, and cook for an additional 2-3 minutes.

4. Push the sweet potato mixture to one side of the skillet and crack the eggs into the empty side.

5. Cook the eggs to your desired doneness, either scrambled or sunny-side-up.

6. Once the eggs are cooked, stir in chopped spinach until wilted.

7. Season the sweet potato hash with salt and pepper to taste.

8. Serve hot, with optional toppings such as avocado slices, salsa, or hot sauce.

Nutritional Information (per serving)

- Calories: 320 kcal

- Protein: 12g

- Fat: 14g

- Carbohydrates: 40g

- Fiber: 8g

- Sugar: 8g

Serving Size: 1 serving

Preparation Time: 10 minutes

Cooking Time: 15 minutes

<table>
<tr><td align="center">NOTE</td></tr>
<tr><td>--</td></tr>
<tr><td>--</td></tr>
<tr><td>--</td></tr>
<tr><td>--</td></tr>
<tr><td>--</td></tr>
<tr><td>--</td></tr>
</table>

10: Banana Walnut Pancakes

Health Benefits

- Bananas provide potassium and vitamin B6, which support nerve function and reduce neuropathic symptoms.

- Walnuts are rich in omega-3 fatty acids and antioxidants, which protect nerve cells from damage and inflammation.

- Whole-wheat flour adds fiber and B vitamins, which support overall nerve health.

Ingredients

- 1 ripe banana, mashed

- 1 cup whole-wheat flour

- 1 tablespoon baking powder

- 1/2 teaspoon cinnamon

- 1/4 teaspoon salt

- Almond milk of 1 Cup (or any milk of your choice)

- 1 egg

- 1/4 cup chopped walnuts

- Optional toppings: sliced bananas, maple syrup, or Greek yogurt

Mode of Preparation

1. In a large mixing bowl, combine mashed banana, whole-wheat flour, baking powder, cinnamon, and salt.

2. In a separate bowl, whisk together almond milk and egg.

3. Wet ingredients should be poured into the dry ingredients and stir until just combined.

4. Fold in chopped walnuts until evenly distributed.

5. Heat a non-stick skillet or griddle over medium heat and lightly grease with cooking spray.

6. 1/4 cup of pancake batter should atleast be poured onto the skillet for each pancake.

7. Cook until bubbles form on the surface, then flip and cook until golden brown on the other side.

8. Repeat with the remaining batter.

9. Serve hot, with optional toppings such as sliced bananas, maple syrup, or Greek yogurt.

Nutritional Information (per serving, 2 pancakes)

- Calories: 300 kcal

- Protein: 10g

- Fat: 10g

- Carbohydrates: 45g

- Fiber: 7g

- Sugar: 8g

Serving Size: 1 serving (2 pancakes)

Preparation Time: 15 minutes

Cooking Time: 10 minutes

<table>
<tr><td>NOTE</td></tr>
<tr><td>

</td></tr>
</table>

CHAPTER 2

Lunch Recipes

1: Grilled Salmon with Quinoa and Steamed Vegetables

Health Benefits

- Salmon is rich in omega-3 fatty acids, which have anti-inflammatory properties and support nerve health.

- Quinoa provides protein, fiber, and magnesium, which help regulate blood sugar levels and support nerve function.

- Steamed vegetables such as broccoli, carrots, and bell peppers are rich in antioxidants and vitamins, which promote overall nerve health.

Ingredients

- 2 salmon fillets (6 ounces each)

- 1 cup quinoa, rinsed

- 2 cups mixed vegetables (broccoli florets, sliced carrots, diced bell peppers)

- 1 tablespoon olive oil

- Salt and pepper to taste

- Lemon wedges for serving

Mode of Preparation

1. Preheat grill to medium-high heat.

2. Season salmon fillets with salt, pepper, and a drizzle of olive oil.

3. Grill salmon for 4-5 minutes per side, or until cooked through and flaky.

4. Cook quinoa according to package instructions, while the salmon is being grilled.

5. In a separate pot, steam mixed vegetables until tender-crisp, about 5-7 minutes.

6. Divide cooked quinoa, grilled salmon, and steamed vegetables evenly among serving plates.

7. Serve with lemon wedges for squeezing over the salmon.

Nutritional Information (per serving)

- Calories: 450 kcal

- Protein: 35g

- Fat: 18g

- Carbohydrates: 35g

- Fiber: 6g

- Sugar: 4g

Serving Size: 1 serving

Preparation Time: 10 minutes

Cooking Time: 20 minutes

2: Chicken and Vegetable Stir-Fry with Brown Rice

Health Benefits

- Chicken is a lean source of protein, which supports muscle and nerve health.

- Brown rice is rich in fiber, B vitamins, and magnesium, which help regulate blood sugar levels and support nerve function.

- Stir-fried vegetables such as bell peppers, broccoli, and snap peas provide antioxidants and vitamins that promote nerve health.

Ingredients

- 2 boneless, skinless chicken breasts, sliced

- 2 cups cooked brown rice

- 2 cups mixed vegetables (sliced bell peppers, broccoli florets, snap peas)

- 2 tablespoons low-sodium soy sauce

- 1 tablespoon olive oil

- 2 cloves garlic, minced

- 1 teaspoon grated ginger

- Salt and pepper to taste

- Optional garnish: chopped green onions, sesame seeds

Mode of Preparation

1. Olive oil should be heated in a large skillet or wok over medium-high heat.

2. Add sliced chicken breast to the skillet and cook until browned and cooked through, about 5-6 minutes.

3. Remove cooked chicken from the skillet and set aside.

4. In the same skillet, add minced garlic and grated ginger, and stir-fry for 1-2 minutes until fragrant.

5. Add mixed vegetables to the skillet and stir-fry until tender-crisp, about 3-4 minutes.

6. Return cooked chicken to the skillet and add cooked brown rice.

7. Drizzle low-sodium soy sauce over the stir-fry and toss to combine.

8. It should be cooked for an additional 2-3 minutes, until everything is heated through.

9. Serve hot, garnished with chopped green onions and sesame seeds if desired.

Nutritional Information (per serving)

- Calories: 400 kcal

- Protein: 30g

- Fat: 8g

- Carbohydrates: 50g

- Fiber: 6g

- Sugar: 4g

Serving Size: 1 serving

Preparation Time: 15 minutes

Cooking Time: 15 minutes

3: Lentil and Vegetable Soup
Health Benefits

- Lentils are rich in protein, fiber, and folate, which support nerve function and reduce inflammation.

- Mixed vegetables such as carrots, celery, and onions provide vitamins, minerals, and antioxidants that promote nerve health.

- Vegetable broth is low in calories and sodium, making it a healthy base for the soup.

Ingredients

- Dried green lentils of 1 Cup, rinsed and drained

- 4 cups low-sodium vegetable broth

- 1 onion, diced

- 2 carrots, diced

- 2 celery stalks, diced

- 2 cloves garlic, minced

- 1 teaspoon dried thyme

- 1 teaspoon dried rosemary

- Salt and pepper to taste

- 2 tablespoons olive oil

- Optional garnish: chopped fresh parsley, lemon wedges

Mode of Preparation

1. Olive oil should be heated in a large pot over medium heat.

2. Add diced onion, carrots, and celery to the pot and sauté until softened, about 5-6 minutes.

3. Stir in minced garlic, dried thyme, and dried rosemary, and cook for an additional 1-2 minutes until fragrant.

4. Add dried lentils and vegetable broth to the pot, and bring to a boil.

5. Reduce heat to low, cover, and simmer for 20-25 minutes, or until lentils are tender.

6. It should be seasoned with salt and pepper to taste.

7. Serve hot, garnished with chopped fresh parsley and lemon wedges if desired.

Nutritional Information (per serving)

- Calories: 300 kcal

- Protein: 15g

- Fat: 6g

- Carbohydrates: 45g

- Fiber: 15g

- Sugar: 6g

Serving Size: 1 serving

Preparation Time: 10 minutes

Cooking Time: 30 minutes

4: Turkey and Quinoa Stuffed Bell Peppers

Health Benefits

- Turkey is a lean source of protein and vitamin B12, which support nerve health and reduce neuropathic symptoms.

- Quinoa provides protein, fiber, and magnesium, which help regulate blood sugar levels and support nerve function.

- Bell peppers are rich in vitamin C and antioxidants, which promote nerve health and reduce inflammation.

Ingredients

- Big Bell pepper (4) of any color halved and seeds removed

- 1 pound lean ground turkey

- 1 cup cooked quinoa

- 1 onion, diced

- 2 cloves garlic, minced

- 1 cup diced tomatoes

- 1 teaspoon dried oregano

- 1 teaspoon paprika

- Salt and pepper to taste

- Shredded cheese, chopped fresh parsley should be as topping but its optional

Mode of Preparation

1. Preheat oven to 375°F (190°C) and grease a baking dish with cooking spray.

2. In a large skillet, cook ground turkey over medium heat until browned and cooked through, breaking it up with a spoon as it cooks.

3. Add diced onion and minced garlic to the skillet, and sauté until softened, about 3-4 minutes.

4. Stir in cooked quinoa, diced tomatoes, dried oregano, paprika, salt, and pepper, and cook for an additional 2-3 minutes.

5. Spoon the turkey-quinoa mixture evenly into the halved bell peppers, pressing down gently to pack the filling.

6. Place stuffed bell peppers in the prepared baking dish and cover with aluminum foil.

7. It should be baked in the preheated oven for 25-30 minutes, or until the peppers are tender.

8. Remove from the oven and garnish with optional shredded cheese and chopped fresh parsley before serving.

Nutritional Information (per serving)

- Calories: 300 kcal

- Protein: 25g

- Fat: 8g

- Carbohydrates: 30g

- Fiber: 7g

- Sugar: 8g

Serving Size: 1 serving (1 stuffed pepper half)

Preparation Time: 20 minutes

Cooking Time: 30 minutes

5: Shrimp and Vegetable Stir-Fry with Quinoa

Health Benefits

- Shrimp is a low-calorie source of protein and omega-3 fatty acids, which support nerve health and reduce inflammation.

- Quinoa provides protein, fiber, and magnesium, which help regulate blood sugar levels and support nerve function.

- Stir-fried vegetables such as bell peppers, snap peas, and mushrooms are rich in antioxidants and vitamins that promote nerve health.

Ingredients

- 1 cup quinoa, rinsed

- Large shrimp of 1 Pound, peeled and deveined

- 2 cups mixed vegetables (sliced bell peppers, snap peas, sliced mushrooms)

- 2 tablespoons low-sodium soy sauce

- 1 tablespoon olive oil

- 2 cloves garlic, minced

- 1 teaspoon grated ginger

- Salt and pepper to taste

- Optional garnish: chopped green onions, sesame seeds

Mode of Preparation

1. Quinoa should be cooked according to package instructions and set aside.

2. Olive oil should be heated in a large skillet or wok over medium-high heat.

3. Add minced garlic and grated ginger to the skillet, and stir-fry for 1-2 minutes until fragrant.

4. Add mixed vegetables to the skillet and stir-fry until tender-crisp, about 3-4 minutes.

5. Push the vegetables to one side of the skillet and add shrimp to the empty side.

6. Cook shrimp for 2-3 minutes per side, or until pink and cooked through.

7. Return cooked quinoa to the skillet and drizzle low-sodium soy sauce over the stir-fry.

8. Toss everything together until evenly combined and heated through.

9. It should be seasoned with salt and pepper to taste.

10. Serve hot, garnished with chopped green onions and sesame seeds if desired.

Nutritional Information (per serving)

- Calories: 350 kcal

- Protein: 30g

- Fat: 8g

- Carbohydrates: 40g

- Fiber: 7g

- Sugar: 4g

Serving Size: 1 serving

Preparation Time: 15 minutes

Cooking Time: 15 minutes

6: Grilled Chicken Caesar Salad

Health Benefits

- Grilled chicken is a lean source of protein, which supports muscle and nerve health.

- Leafy greens like romaine lettuce provide vitamins, minerals, and antioxidants that promote nerve health and reduce inflammation.

- Parmesan cheese adds calcium and protein, which are important for nerve function and bone health.

Ingredients

- 2 boneless, skinless chicken breasts

- 6 cups chopped romaine lettuce

- 1/4 cup grated Parmesan cheese

- 1/4 cup Caesar salad dressing (low-sodium if possible)

- Salt and pepper to taste

- Optional toppings: croutons, cherry tomatoes, sliced cucumbers

Mode of Preparation

1. Preheat grill to medium-high heat.

2. Season chicken breasts with salt and pepper.

3. Grill chicken for 6-8 minutes per side, or until cooked through and no longer pink in the center.

4. Let the chicken rest for a few minutes, then slice it thinly.

5. In a large bowl, combine chopped romaine lettuce, sliced grilled chicken, grated Parmesan cheese, and Caesar salad dressing.

6. Toss until evenly coated.

7. Serve immediately, garnished with optional toppings if desired.

Nutritional Information (per serving)

- Calories: 350 kcal

- Protein: 35g

- Fat: 15g

- Carbohydrates: 15g

- Fiber: 5g

- Sugar: 3g

Serving Size: 1 serving

Preparation Time: 10 minutes

Cooking Time: 15 minutes

7: Lentil Salad with Mixed Greens and Balsamic Vinaigrette

Health Benefits

- Lentils are rich in protein, fiber, and folate, which support nerve function and reduce inflammation.

- Mixed greens like spinach and arugula provide vitamins, minerals, and antioxidants that promote nerve health and reduce oxidative stress.

- Balsamic vinaigrette adds flavor and healthy fats from olive oil, which support heart and nerve health.

Ingredients

- 1 cup cooked lentils

- Mixed greens of 4 cups (spinach, arugula, kale)

- 1/4 cup cherry tomatoes, halved

- 1/4 cup diced cucumber

- 2 tablespoons crumbled feta cheese

- 2 tablespoons balsamic vinaigrette

- Salt and pepper to taste

- Optional toppings: sliced almonds, dried cranberries

Mode of Preparation

1. In a large bowl, combine cooked lentils, mixed greens, cherry tomatoes, diced cucumber, and crumbled feta cheese.

2. Drizzle balsamic vinaigrette over the salad and toss until evenly coated.

3. It should be seasoned with salt and pepper to taste.

4. Serve immediately, garnished with optional toppings if desired.

Nutritional Information (per serving)

- Calories: 300 kcal

- Protein: 15g

- Fat: 10g

- Carbohydrates: 40g

- Fiber: 15g

- Sugar: 5g

Serving Size: 1 serving

Preparation Time: 10 minutes

<table>
<tr><td align="center">NOTE</td></tr>
<tr><td>

</td></tr>
</table>

8: Turkey and Vegetable Wrap

Health Benefits

- Turkey is a lean source of protein and vitamin B12, which support nerve health and reduce neuropathic symptoms.

- Whole-grain wraps provide fiber and B vitamins, which support digestive and nerve health.

- Mixed vegetables like bell peppers, spinach, and carrots provide vitamins, minerals, and antioxidants that promote nerve health and reduce inflammation.

Ingredients

- 4 whole-grain wraps or tortillas

- 8 ounces sliced turkey breast

- 1 cup mixed vegetables (sliced bell peppers, spinach leaves, shredded carrots)

- 1/4 cup hummus or Greek yogurt spread

- Salt and pepper to taste

- Optional add-ins: sliced avocado, shredded cheese, sprouts

Mode of Preparation

1. Whole-grain should be laid out wraps on a flat surface.

2. Spread hummus or Greek yogurt spread evenly over each wrap.

3. Layer sliced turkey breast and mixed vegetables on top of the spread.

4. It should be seasoned with salt and pepper to taste.

5. Add any optional add-ins such as sliced avocado, shredded cheese, or sprouts.

6. Roll up the wraps tightly and slice in half diagonally.

7. Serve immediately, or wrap in foil for later.

Nutritional Information (per serving)

- Calories: 300 kcal

- Protein: 20g

- Fat: 10g

- Carbohydrates: 30g

- Fiber: 8g

- Sugar: 4g

Serving Size: 1 wrap

Preparation Time: 10 minutes

Cooking Time: 0 minutes

9: Quinoa and Black Bean Salad with Avocado Dressing

Health Benefits

- Quinoa provides protein, fiber, and magnesium, which help regulate blood sugar levels and support nerve function.

- Black beans are rich in protein, fiber, and folate, which support nerve health and reduce neuropathic symptoms.

- Avocado dressing adds healthy fats and vitamins, which promote nerve health and reduce inflammation.

Ingredients

- 1 cup cooked quinoa

- Black beans of 1 can (15 ounces), rinsed and drained

- 1 cup corn kernels (fresh, canned, or frozen)

- 1/4 cup diced red onion

- 1/4 cup chopped cilantro

- 1 ripe avocado

- 1/4 cup plain Greek yogurt

- 1 tablespoon lime juice

- Salt and pepper to taste

- Optional toppings: diced tomatoes, sliced jalapenos, tortilla strips

Mode of Preparation

1. In a large bowl, combine cooked quinoa, black beans, corn kernels, diced red onion, and chopped cilantro.

2. In a blender or food processor, combine ripe avocado, plain Greek yogurt, lime juice, salt, and pepper.

3. Blend until smooth and creamy, adding water as needed to reach desired consistency.

4. Pour the avocado dressing over the quinoa salad and toss until evenly coated.

5. Serve immediately, garnished with optional toppings if desired.

Nutritional Information (per serving)

- Calories: 350 kcal

- Protein: 15g

- Fat: 15g

- Carbohydrates: 40g

- Fiber: 12g

- Sugar: 5g

Serving Size: 1 serving

Preparation Time: 15 minutes

10: Veggie and Hummus Wrap

Health Benefits

- Whole-grain wraps provide fiber and B vitamins, which support digestive and nerve health.

- Hummus is made from chickpeas, which are rich in protein, fiber, and folate, supporting nerve health and reducing inflammation.

- Mixed vegetables like spinach, bell peppers, and cucumbers provide vitamins, minerals, and antioxidants that promote nerve health and reduce oxidative stress.

Ingredients

- 4 whole-grain wraps or tortillas

- 1 cup hummus (store-bought or homemade)

- 2 cups mixed vegetables (spinach leaves, sliced bell peppers, sliced cucumbers)

- Salt and pepper to taste

- Optional add-ins: sliced avocado, shredded carrots, feta cheese

Mode of Preparation

1. Whole-grain wraps should be laid on a flat surface.

2. Spread hummus evenly over each wrap, leaving a small border around the edges.

3. Layer mixed vegetables on top of the hummus.

4. It should be seasoned with salt and pepper to taste.

5. Add any optional add-ins such as sliced avocado, shredded carrots, or crumbled feta cheese.

6. Roll up the wraps tightly and slice in half diagonally.

7. Serve immediately or wrap in foil for later.

Nutritional Information (per serving)

- Calories: 300 kcal

- Protein: 10g

- Fat: 12g

- Carbohydrates: 40g

- Fiber: 10g

- Sugar: 5g

Serving Size: 1 wrap

Preparation Time: 10 minutes

<table><tr><td align="center">NOTE</td></tr></table>

CHAPTER 3

Dinner Recipes

1: Baked Salmon with Roasted Vegetables

Health Benefits

- Salmon is rich in omega-3 fatty acids, which have anti-inflammatory properties and support nerve health.

- Roasted vegetables such as carrots, bell peppers, and zucchini provide vitamins, minerals, and antioxidants that promote nerve health and reduce inflammation.

- Olive oil used for roasting vegetables contains healthy fats and antioxidants, further supporting nerve health.

Ingredients

- 2 salmon fillets (6 ounces each)

- 2 cups mixed vegetables (carrots, bell peppers, zucchini), cut into bite-sized pieces

- 2 tablespoons olive oil

- Salt and pepper to taste

- Optional seasoning: garlic powder, dried herbs (such as thyme or rosemary)

Mode of Preparation

1. Oven should be preheated to 400°F (200°C) and line a baking sheet with parchment paper.

2. Place salmon fillets on one side of the baking sheet and arrange mixed vegetables on the other side.

3. Drizzle olive oil over the salmon and vegetables, then season with salt, pepper, and optional seasonings.

4. Toss the vegetables to coat evenly with oil and seasoning.

5. Bake in the preheated oven for 15-20 minutes, or until salmon is cooked through and vegetables are tender.

6. It should be removed from the oven and serve hot.

Nutritional Information (per serving)

- Calories: 350 kcal

- Protein: 30g

- Fat: 20g

- Carbohydrates: 10g

- Fiber: 3g

- Sugar: 4g

Serving Size: 1 serving

Preparation Time: 10 minutes

Cooking Time: 20 minutes

2: Quinoa Stuffed Bell Peppers

Health Benefits

- Quinoa provides protein, fiber, and magnesium, which help regulate blood sugar levels and support nerve function.

- Bell peppers are rich in vitamin C and antioxidants, which promote nerve health and reduce inflammation.

- Lean ground turkey adds protein and vitamin B12, which support nerve health and reduce neuropathic symptoms.

Ingredients

- Big Bell pepper (4) of any color halved and seeds removed

- 1 cup cooked quinoa

- 1/2 pound lean ground turkey

- 1 onion, diced

- 1 clove garlic, minced

- 1 cup diced tomatoes

- 1 teaspoon dried oregano

- Salt and pepper to taste

- Optional toppings: shredded cheese, chopped parsley

Mode of Preparation

1. Preheat oven to 375°F (190°C) and grease a baking dish with cooking spray.

2. In a large skillet, cook ground turkey over medium heat until browned and cooked through, breaking it up with a spoon as it cooks.

3. Add diced onion and minced garlic to the skillet, and sauté until softened, about 3-4 minutes.

4. Stir in diced tomatoes, cooked quinoa, dried oregano, salt, and pepper, and cook for an additional 2-3 minutes.

5. Spoon the turkey-quinoa mixture evenly into the halved bell peppers, pressing down gently to pack the filling.

6. Place stuffed bell peppers in the prepared baking dish and cover with aluminum foil.

7. It should be baked in the preheated oven for 25-30 minutes, or until the peppers are tender.

8. Remove from the oven and garnish with optional shredded cheese and chopped parsley before serving.

Nutritional Information (per serving)

- Calories: 300 kcal

- Protein: 25g

- Fat: 8g

- Carbohydrates: 30g

- Fiber: 7g

- Sugar: 8g

Serving Size: 1 serving (1 stuffed pepper half)

Preparation Time: 20 minutes

Cooking Time: 30 minutes

3: Vegetable and Lentil Curry

Health Benefits

- Lentils are rich in protein, fiber, and folate, which support nerve function and reduce inflammation.

- Mixed vegetables like carrots, bell peppers, and spinach provide vitamins, minerals, and antioxidants that promote nerve health and reduce oxidative stress.

- Coconut milk used in the curry adds healthy fats and flavor, supporting nerve health and reducing inflammation.

Ingredients

- Dried green lentils of 1 Cup, rinsed and drained

- 4 cups low-sodium vegetable broth

- 1 onion, diced

- 2 cloves garlic, minced

- 1 tablespoon grated ginger

- 2 teaspoons curry powder

- 1 can (14 ounces) coconut milk

- 2 cups mixed vegetables (carrots, bell peppers, spinach), chopped

- Salt and pepper to taste

- Optional garnish: chopped cilantro, lime wedges

Mode of Preparation

1. In a large pot, combine dried lentils and vegetable broth, and bring to a boil.

2. Reduce heat to low, cover, and simmer for 20-25 minutes, or until lentils are tender.

3. Olive oil should be heated in a separate skillet over medium heat.

4. Add diced onion, minced garlic, and grated ginger to the skillet, and sauté until softened, about 3-4 minutes.

5. Stir in curry powder and cook for an additional 1-2 minutes until fragrant.

6. Add coconut milk and mixed vegetables to the skillet, and simmer for 5-7 minutes, or until vegetables are tender.

7. Once the lentils are cooked, add the vegetable-coconut milk mixture to the pot, and stir to combine.

8. It should be seasoned with salt and pepper to taste.

9. Serve hot, garnished with chopped cilantro and lime wedges if desired.

Nutritional Information (per serving)

- Calories: 350 kcal

- Protein: 15g

- Fat: 20g

- Carbohydrates: 35g

- Fiber: 10g

- Sugar: 5g

Serving Size: 1 serving

Preparation Time: 10 minutes

Cooking Time: 30 minutes

4: Vegetable Stir-Fry and Chicken with Brown Rice
Health Benefits

- Chicken is a lean source of protein, which supports muscle and nerve health.

- Brown rice is rich in fiber, B vitamins, and magnesium, which help regulate blood sugar levels and support nerve function.

- Stir-fried vegetables such as bell peppers, broccoli, and snap peas provide antioxidants and vitamins that promote nerve health.

Ingredients

- 2 boneless, skinless chicken breasts, sliced

- 2 cups cooked brown rice

- 2 cups mixed vegetables (sliced bell peppers, broccoli florets, snap peas)

- 2 tablespoons low-sodium soy sauce

- 1 tablespoon olive oil

- 2 cloves garlic, minced

- 1 teaspoon grated ginger

- Salt and pepper to taste

- Optional garnish: chopped green onions, sesame seeds

Mode of Preparation

1. Olive oil should be heated in a large skillet or wok over medium-high heat.

2. Add sliced chicken breast to the skillet and cook until browned and cooked through, about 5-6 minutes.

3. Remove cooked chicken from the skillet and set aside.

4. In the same skillet, add minced garlic and grated ginger, and stir-fry for 1-2 minutes until fragrant.

5. Add mixed vegetables to the skillet and stir-fry until tender-crisp, about 3-4 minutes.

6. Return cooked chicken to the skillet and add cooked brown rice.

7. Drizzle low-sodium soy sauce over the stir-fry and toss to combine.

8. It should be cooked for an additional 2-3 minutes, until everything is heated through.

9. Serve hot, garnished with chopped green onions and sesame seeds if desired.

Nutritional Information (per serving)

- Calories: 400 kcal

- Protein: 30g

- Fat: 8g

- Carbohydrates: 50g

- Fiber: 6g

- Sugar: 4g

Serving Size: 1 serving

Preparation Time: 15 minutes

Cooking Time: 15 minutes

5: Veggie and Tofu Stir-Fry with Quinoa

Health Benefits

- Tofu is a plant-based source of protein, which supports muscle and nerve health.

- Quinoa provides protein, fiber, and magnesium, which help regulate blood sugar levels and support nerve function.

- Stir-fried vegetables such as bell peppers, snap peas, and mushrooms are rich in antioxidants and vitamins that promote nerve health.

Ingredients

- 1 cup quinoa, rinsed

- Firm tofu of 1 package (14 ounces), drained and cubed

- 2 cups mixed vegetables (sliced bell peppers, snap peas, sliced mushrooms)

- 2 tablespoons low-sodium soy sauce

- 1 tablespoon olive oil

- 2 cloves garlic, minced

- 1 teaspoon grated ginger

- Salt and pepper to taste

- Optional garnish: chopped green onions, sesame seeds

Mode of Preparation

1. Quinoa should be cooked according to package instructions and set aside.

2. Olive oil should be heated in a large skillet or wok over medium-high heat.

3. Add cubed tofu to the skillet and cook until golden brown on all sides, about 5-6 minutes.

4. Cooked tofu should be removed from the skillet and set aside.

5. In the same skillet, add minced garlic and grated ginger, and stir-fry for 1-2 minutes until fragrant.

6. Add mixed vegetables to the skillet and stir-fry until tender-crisp, about 3-4 minutes.

7. Return cooked tofu to the skillet and add cooked quinoa.

8. Drizzle low-sodium soy sauce over the stir-fry and toss to combine.

9. It should be cooked for an additional 2-3 minutes, until everything is heated through.

10. Serve hot, garnished with chopped green onions and sesame seeds if desired.

Nutritional Information (per serving)

- Calories: 350 kcal

- Protein: 25g

- Fat: 15g

- Carbohydrates: 40g

- Fiber: 7g

- Sugar: 4g

Serving Size: 1 serving

Preparation Time: 15 minutes

Cooking Time: 15 minutes

6: Baked Chicken with Sweet Potato Mash and Steamed Broccoli
Health Benefits

- Chicken is a lean source of protein, essential for muscle and nerve health.

- Sweet potatoes are rich in fiber, vitamins, and antioxidants, promoting nerve health and reducing inflammation.

- Broccoli is packed with vitamins, minerals, and antioxidants, supporting overall nerve health and reducing oxidative stress.

Ingredients

- 2 boneless, skinless chicken breasts

- 2 Sweet potatoes of medium size, peeled and cubed

- 2 cups broccoli florets

- 2 tablespoons olive oil

- Salt and pepper to taste

- Optional seasoning for chicken: garlic powder, paprika, thyme

Mode of Preparation

1. Preheat oven to 400°F (200°C).

2. Chicken breasts should be placed on a baking sheet lined with parchment paper.

3. Drizzle olive oil over the chicken breasts and season with salt, pepper, and optional seasonings.

4. Bake chicken in the preheated oven for 20-25 minutes, or until cooked through and no longer pink in the center.

5. While the chicken is baking, steam broccoli florets until tender.

6. In a separate pot, boil sweet potato cubes until soft, then drain.

7. Mash the cooked sweet potatoes with a fork or potato masher until smooth.

8. Season sweet potato mash with salt and pepper to taste.

9. Serve baked chicken with a side of sweet potato mash and steamed broccoli.

Nutritional Information (per serving)

- Calories: 400 kcal

- Protein: 30g

- Fat: 10g

- Carbohydrates: 45g

- Fiber: 8g

- Sugar: 10g

Serving Size: 1 serving

Preparation Time: 15 minutes

Cooking Time: 25 minutes

7: Turkey Chili with Black Beans and Bell Peppers

Health Benefits

- Lean ground turkey is a rich source of protein, essential for muscle and nerve health.

- Black beans provide protein, fiber, and folate, supporting nerve function and reducing inflammation.

- Bell peppers are packed with vitamin C and antioxidants, promoting nerve health and reducing oxidative stress.

Ingredients

- 1 pound lean ground turkey

- 1 onion, diced

- 2 cloves garlic, minced

- 1 bell pepper, diced

- Black beans of 1 can (15 ounces) , rinsed and drained

- 1 can (14 ounces) diced tomatoes

- 2 cups low-sodium chicken broth

- 2 tablespoons chili powder

- 1 teaspoon ground cumin

- Salt and pepper to taste

- Optional toppings: shredded cheese, diced avocado, chopped cilantro

Mode of Preparation

1. In a large pot or Dutch oven, cook ground turkey over medium heat until browned and cooked through.

2. Add diced onion, minced garlic, and diced bell pepper to the pot, and sauté until softened, about 5 minutes.

3. Stir in chili powder and ground cumin, and cook for an additional 1-2 minutes until fragrant.

4. Add black beans, diced tomatoes, and chicken broth to the pot, and bring to a simmer.

5. Reduce heat to low, cover, and simmer for 20-25 minutes, stirring occasionally.

6. It should be seasoned with salt and pepper to taste.

7. Serve hot, garnished with optional toppings if desired.

Nutritional Information (per serving)

- Calories: 350 kcal

- Protein: 30g

- Fat: 10g

- Carbohydrates: 35g

- Fiber: 10g

- Sugar: 5g

Serving Size: 1 serving

Preparation Time: 15 minutes

Cooking Time: 30 minutes

8: Veggie and Chickpea Curry with Brown Rice

Health Benefits

- Chickpeas are high in protein, fiber, and folate, supporting nerve health and reducing inflammation.

- Mixed vegetables like carrots, bell peppers, and spinach provide vitamins, minerals, and antioxidants that promote nerve health and reduce oxidative stress.

- Brown rice is rich in fiber, B vitamins, and magnesium, supporting blood sugar regulation and nerve function.

Ingredients

- 1 cup cooked brown rice

- 1 can (15 ounces) chickpeas, rinsed and drained

- 2 cups mixed vegetables (carrots, bell peppers, spinach), chopped

- 1 onion, diced

- 2 cloves garlic, minced

- 1 tablespoon curry powder

- 1 can (14 ounces) coconut milk

- 2 tablespoons olive oil

- Salt and pepper to taste

- Optional garnish: chopped cilantro, lime wedges

Mode of Preparation

1. Olive oil should be heated in a large skillet over medium heat.

2. Add diced onion and minced garlic to the skillet, and sauté until softened, about 3-4 minutes.

3. Stir in curry powder and cook for an additional 1-2 minutes until fragrant.

4. Add mixed vegetables to the skillet and stir-fry until tender-crisp, about 3-4 minutes.

5. Add chickpeas and coconut milk to the skillet, and bring to a simmer.

6. Reduce heat to low, cover, and simmer for 10-15 minutes, stirring occasionally.

7. It should be seasoned with salt and pepper to taste.

8. Serve hot, spooned over cooked brown rice.

9. Garnish with chopped cilantro and lime wedges if desired.

Nutritional Information (per serving)

- Calories: 400 kcal

- Protein: 15g

- Fat: 20g

- Carbohydrates: 45g

- Fiber: 10g

- Sugar: 5g

Serving Size: 1 serving

Preparation Time: 15 minutes

Cooking Time: 25 minutes

9: Grilled Vegetable and Chicken Skewers with Quinoa

Health Benefits

- Chicken is a lean source of protein, essential for muscle and nerve health.

- Grilled vegetables such as bell peppers, zucchini, and cherry tomatoes are rich in vitamins, minerals, and antioxidants, promoting nerve health and reducing inflammation.

- Quinoa provides protein, fiber, and magnesium, supporting blood sugar regulation and nerve function.

Ingredients

- Boneless and skinless chicken breasts (2), cut into cubes

- 2 cups cooked quinoa

- 2 cups mixed vegetables (bell peppers, zucchini, cherry tomatoes), cut into bite-sized pieces

- 2 tablespoons olive oil

- Salt and pepper to taste

- Wooden skewers, soaked in water for 30 minutes

Mode of Preparation

1. Preheat grill to medium-high heat.

2. Thread chicken cubes and mixed vegetables onto the soaked wooden skewers, alternating between chicken and vegetables.

3. Brush olive oil over the skewers and season with salt and pepper.

4. Grill skewers for 8-10 minutes, turning occasionally, until chicken is cooked through and vegetables are tender.

5. Remove skewers from the grill and serve hot, accompanied by cooked quinoa.

Nutritional Information (per serving)

- Calories: 350 kcal

- Protein: 25g

- Fat: 10g

- Carbohydrates: 40g

- Fiber: 8g

- Sugar: 4g

Serving Size: 1 serving

Preparation Time: 15 minutes

Cooking Time: 10 minutes

10: Spinach and Feta Stuffed Chicken Breast

Health Benefits

- Chicken breast is a lean source of protein, essential for muscle and nerve health.

- Spinach is rich in vitamins, minerals, and antioxidants, promoting nerve health and reducing inflammation.

- Feta cheese adds calcium and protein, supporting nerve function and bone health.

Ingredients

- 2 boneless, skinless chicken breasts

- 2 cups fresh spinach leaves

- 1/4 cup crumbled feta cheese

- 2 cloves garlic, minced

- 1 tablespoon olive oil

- Salt and pepper to taste

- Toothpicks or kitchen twine

Mode of Preparation

1. Preheat oven to 375°F (190°C) and grease a baking dish with cooking spray.

2. Olive oil should be heated in a skillet over medium heat.

3. Add minced garlic to the skillet and sauté until fragrant, about 1 minute.

4. Add spinach leaves to the skillet and cook until wilted, about 2-3 minutes.

5. Remove spinach from the skillet and let it cool slightly.

6. Butterfly each chicken breast by slicing horizontally, but not all the way through, to create a pocket.

7. Stuff each chicken breast with cooked spinach and crumbled feta cheese.

8. Use toothpicks or kitchen twine to secure the stuffed chicken breasts closed.

9. Season the stuffed chicken breasts with salt and pepper.

10. Place stuffed chicken breasts in the prepared baking dish and bake in the preheated oven for 25-30 minutes, or until chicken is cooked through and no longer pink in the center.

11. It should be removed from the oven and let it rest for a few minutes before serving.

Nutritional Information (per serving)

- Calories: 300 kcal

- Protein: 30g

- Fat: 12g

- Carbohydrates: 5g

- Fiber: 2g

- Sugar: 1g

Serving Size: 1 stuffed chicken breast

Preparation Time: 20 minutes

Cooking Time: 25-30 minutes

<table>
<tr><td align="center">NOTE</td></tr>
<tr><td>--</td></tr>
<tr><td>--</td></tr>
<tr><td>--</td></tr>
<tr><td>--</td></tr>
<tr><td>--</td></tr>
<tr><td>--</td></tr>
<tr><td>--</td></tr>
<tr><td>--</td></tr>
<tr><td>--</td></tr>
<tr><td>--</td></tr>
<tr><td>--</td></tr>
<tr><td>--</td></tr>
</table>

CHAPTER 4

Snacks and Appetizers

1: Avocado and Black Bean Salsa

Health Benefits

- Avocado is rich in healthy fats, vitamins, and antioxidants, promoting nerve health and reducing inflammation.

- Black beans provide protein, fiber, and folate, supporting nerve function and reducing neuropathic symptoms.

Ingredients

- 1 ripe avocado, diced

- Black beans of 1 can (15 ounces) , rinsed and drained

- 1/2 cup diced tomatoes

- 1/4 cup diced red onion

- 1/4 cup chopped cilantro

- Jalapeno pepper (1), seeded and minced (optional)

- Juice of 1 lime

- Salt and pepper to taste

- Optional: tortilla chips or cucumber slices for serving

Mode of Preparation

1. In a large bowl, combine diced avocado, black beans, diced tomatoes, diced red onion, chopped cilantro, and minced jalapeno pepper (if using).

2. Lime juice should be squeezed over the mixture and toss gently to combine.

3. It should be seasoned with salt and pepper to taste.

4. Serve immediately with tortilla chips or cucumber slices for dipping.

Nutritional Information (per serving, without chips)

- Calories: 150 kcal

- Protein: 6g

- Fat: 7g

- Carbohydrates: 18g

- Fiber: 7g

- Sugar: 1g

Serving Size: 1/2 cup salsa

Preparation Time: 10 minutes

2: Greek Yogurt and Berry Parfait

Health Benefits

- Greek yogurt is high in protein and probiotics, supporting digestive and nerve health.

- Berries such as strawberries, blueberries, and raspberries are rich in antioxidants and vitamins, promoting nerve health and reducing oxidative stress.

Ingredients

- 1 cup plain Greek yogurt

- 1/2 cup mixed berries (strawberries, blueberries, raspberries)

- 2 tablespoons chopped nuts (almonds, walnuts, or pecans)

- Honey or maple syrup of 1 tablespoon (optional)

Mode of Preparation

1. In a serving glass or bowl, layer plain Greek yogurt, mixed berries, and chopped nuts.

2. Drizzle honey or maple syrup over the top if desired.

3. Repeat the layers until the glass or bowl is filled.

4. Serve immediately as a nutritious snack or dessert.

Nutritional Information (per serving)

- Calories: 200 kcal

- Protein: 15g

- Fat: 8g

- Carbohydrates: 20g

- Fiber: 4g

- Sugar: 12g

Serving Size: 1 serving

Preparation Time: 5 minutes

3: Hummus and Veggie Platter

Health Benefits

- Hummus is made from chickpeas, which are high in protein, fiber, and folate, supporting nerve health and reducing inflammation.

- Mixed vegetables such as carrots, cucumber, and bell peppers provide vitamins, minerals, and antioxidants, promoting nerve health and reducing oxidative stress.

Ingredients

- 1 cup hummus (store-bought or homemade)

- 2 carrots, peeled and sliced into sticks

- 1 cucumber, sliced

- 1 bell pepper, sliced

- Optional: cherry tomatoes, celery sticks, broccoli florets

Mode of Preparation

1. Arrange hummus in a serving bowl or platter.

2. Surround the hummus with sliced carrots, cucumber, bell pepper, and any other desired vegetables.

3. Serve immediately as a nutritious snack or appetizer.

Nutritional Information (per serving)

- Calories: 200 kcal

- Protein: 8g

- Fat: 10g

- Carbohydrates: 20g

- Fiber: 8g

- Sugar: 5g

Serving Size: 1 serving

Preparation Time: 10 minutes

4: Almond Butter and Banana Toast

Health Benefits

- Almond butter is rich in healthy fats, protein, and magnesium, supporting nerve health and reducing neuropathic symptoms.

- Bananas are a good source of potassium and vitamin B6, which promote nerve health and reduce inflammation.

Ingredients

- 2 slices whole-grain bread, toasted

- 2 tablespoons almond butter

- 1 banana, sliced

- Honey should be drizzle or sprinkle of cinnamon

Mode of Preparation

1. Spread almond butter evenly over each slice of toasted whole-grain bread.

2. Arrange sliced banana on top of the almond butter.

3. Drizzle honey or sprinkle cinnamon over the bananas if desired.

4. Serve immediately as a quick and satisfying snack.

Nutritional Information (per serving)

- Calories: 300 kcal

- Protein: 8g

- Fat: 15g

- Carbohydrates: 35g

- Fiber: 7g

- Sugar: 10g

Serving Size: 1 serving

Preparation Time: 5 minutes

5: Spinach and Feta Stuffed Mushrooms

Health Benefits

- Spinach is rich in vitamins, minerals, and antioxidants, promoting nerve health and reducing inflammation.

- Feta cheese adds calcium and protein, supporting nerve function and bone health.

- Mushrooms provide B vitamins and antioxidants, promoting nerve health and reducing oxidative stress.

Ingredients

- 8 large mushrooms, stems removed

- 1 cup fresh spinach leaves, chopped

- 1/4 cup crumbled feta cheese

- 2 cloves garlic, minced

- 1 tablespoon olive oil

- Salt and pepper to taste

Mode of Preparation

1. Preheat oven to 375°F (190°C) and grease a baking dish with cooking spray.

2. Olive oil should be heated in a skillet over medium heat.

3. Add minced garlic to the skillet and sauté until fragrant, about 1 minute.

4. Add chopped spinach to the skillet and cook until wilted, about 2-3 minutes.

5. Remove skillet from heat and stir in crumbled feta cheese.

6. Spoon the spinach and feta mixture into the mushroom caps, dividing evenly.

7. Place stuffed mushrooms in the prepared baking dish and bake in the preheated oven for 15-20 minutes, or until mushrooms are tender.

8. It should be seasoned with salt and pepper to taste.

9. Serve hot as a flavorful snack or appetizer.

Nutritional Information (per serving)

- Calories: 100 kcal

- Protein: 5g

- Fat: 7g

- Carbohydrates: 5g

- Fiber: 2g

- Sugar: 2g

Serving Size: 2 stuffed mushrooms

Preparation Time: 10 minutes

Cooking Time: 20 minutes

6: Cucumber and Smoked Salmon Rolls

Health Benefits

- Cucumbers are hydrating and low in calories, providing vitamins and minerals that support nerve health.

- Smoked salmon is rich in omega-3 fatty acids, which have anti-inflammatory properties and support nerve function.

Ingredients

- 1 English cucumber

- 4 ounces smoked salmon

- Cream cheese or Greek yogurt of 1/4 cup

- 1 tablespoon fresh dill, chopped

- 1 teaspoon lemon juice

- Salt and pepper to taste

Mode of Preparation

1. Using a mandoline or vegetable peeler, slice the cucumber lengthwise into thin strips.

2. In a small bowl, mix cream cheese or Greek yogurt with chopped fresh dill and lemon juice.

3. Spread a thin layer of the cream cheese mixture onto each cucumber strip.

4. Slice of smoked salmon should be placed on top of the cream cheese mixture.

5. Roll up the cucumber strips with smoked salmon.

6. Secure the rolls with toothpicks if necessary.

7. Serve chilled as a refreshing and nutritious appetizer.

Nutritional Information (per serving)

- Calories: 100 kcal

- Protein: 8g

- Fat: 5g

- Carbohydrates: 5g

- Fiber: 1g

- Sugar: 2g

Serving Size: 4 rolls

Preparation Time: 15 minutes

Cooking Time: 0 minutes

7: Edamame and Snap Pea Salad

Health Benefits

- Edamame is a good source of plant-based protein, fiber, and folate, supporting nerve health and reducing neuropathic symptoms.

- Snap peas are low in calories and high in fiber and antioxidants, promoting nerve health and reducing oxidative stress.

Ingredients

- 2 cups cooked edamame

- 1 cup snap peas, sliced

- 1/4 cup red onion, thinly sliced

- 2 tablespoons fresh mint leaves, chopped

- 1 tablespoon sesame seeds

- 2 tablespoons rice vinegar

- 1 tablespoon low-sodium soy sauce

- 1 teaspoon honey or maple syrup

- Salt and pepper to taste

Mode of Preparation

1. In a large bowl, combine cooked edamame, sliced snap peas, thinly sliced red onion, and chopped fresh mint leaves.

2. In a separate small bowl, whisk together rice vinegar, low-sodium soy sauce, honey or maple syrup, salt, and pepper to make the dressing.

3. Dressing should be poured over the salad and toss to combine.

4. Sprinkle sesame seeds over the salad before serving.

5. Serve chilled as a refreshing and nutritious snack or side dish.

Nutritional Information (per serving)

- Calories: 150 kcal

- Protein: 10g

- Fat: 5g

- Carbohydrates: 15g

- Fiber: 6g

- Sugar: 5g

Serving Size: 1 cup

Preparation Time: 10 minutes

Cooking Time: 5 minutes

8: Stuffed Bell Pepper Bites

Health Benefits

- Bell peppers are low in calories and high in vitamins and antioxidants, promoting nerve health and reducing inflammation.

- Cream cheese provides protein and healthy fats, supporting nerve function and reducing neuropathic symptoms.

Ingredients

- 2 bell peppers (any color)

- 4 ounces cream cheese, softened

- 1/4 cup chopped olives or sundried tomatoes

- 2 tablespoons chopped fresh parsley

- Salt and pepper to taste

Mode of Preparation

1. Slice bell peppers into thick rings, discarding the seeds and membranes.

2. In a small bowl, mix softened cream cheese with chopped olives or sundried tomatoes, chopped fresh parsley, salt, and pepper.

3. Spoon the cream cheese mixture into each bell pepper ring, filling them evenly.

4. Arrange stuffed bell pepper bites on a serving platter.

5. Serve immediately as a delicious and nutritious appetizer.

Nutritional Information (per serving)

- Calories: 100 kcal

- Protein: 3g

- Fat: 8g

- Carbohydrates: 5g

- Fiber: 1g

- Sugar: 2g

Serving Size: 4 stuffed pepper rings

Preparation Time: 15 minutes

9: Caprese Skewers

Health Benefits

- Tomatoes are rich in vitamins and antioxidants, promoting nerve health and reducing oxidative stress.

- Fresh mozzarella cheese provides protein and calcium, supporting nerve function and bone health.

- Basil contains essential oils and antioxidants that promote nerve health and reduce inflammation.

Ingredients

- 1 cup cherry tomatoes

- 1 cup fresh mozzarella balls (bocconcini)

- Fresh basil leaves

- Balsamic glaze for drizzling

- Wooden skewers

Mode of Preparation

1. Thread cherry tomatoes, fresh mozzarella balls, and fresh basil leaves onto wooden skewers, alternating between ingredients.

2. Caprese skewers should be arranged on a serving platter.

3. Drizzle balsamic glaze over the skewers before serving.

4. Serve immediately as a simple and elegant appetizer.

Nutritional Information (per serving)

- Calories: 150 kcal

- Protein: 8g

- Fat: 10g

- Carbohydrates: 5g

- Fiber: 1g

- Sugar: 2g

Serving Size: 4 skewers

Preparation Time: 10 minutes

10: Quinoa-Stuffed Mini Peppers

Health Benefits

- Quinoa is a gluten-free whole grain rich in protein, fiber, and essential vitamins and minerals, supporting nerve health and reducing neuropathic symptoms.

- Mini bell peppers are low in calories and high in vitamins and antioxidants, promoting nerve health and reducing inflammation.

Ingredients

- 1/2 cup cooked quinoa

- 8-10 mini bell peppers, halved and seeded

- 1/4 cup black beans, rinsed and drained

- Corn kernels of 1/4 cup (fresh or frozen)

- 1/4 cup diced tomatoes

- 2 tablespoons chopped cilantro

- 1 tablespoon lime juice

- Salt and pepper to taste

Mode of Preparation

1. Oven should be pre heated to 375°F (190°C) and line a baking sheet with parchment paper.

2. In a large bowl, combine cooked quinoa, black beans, corn kernels, diced tomatoes, chopped cilantro, lime juice, salt, and pepper.

3. Spoon the quinoa mixture into each halved mini bell pepper, filling them evenly.

4. Place stuffed mini peppers on the prepared baking sheet.

5. Bake in the preheated oven for 15-20 minutes, or until peppers are tender.

6. Serve hot as a flavorful and nutritious appetizer.

Nutritional Information (per serving)

- Calories: 100 kcal

- Protein: 4g

- Fat: 1g

- Carbohydrates: 20g

- Fiber: 4g

- Sugar: 2g

Serving Size: 4 stuffed mini peppers

Preparation Time: 15 minutes

Cooking Time: 20 minutes

<table>
<tr><td align="center">NOTE</td></tr>
</table>

CHAPTER 5

Smoothies

1: Berry Blast

Health Benefits

- Berries such as strawberries, blueberries, and raspberries are rich in antioxidants and vitamins that promote nerve health and reduce oxidative stress.

- Spinach is high in folate and magnesium, supporting nerve function and reducing neuropathic symptoms.

- Greek yogurt provides protein and probiotics, supporting digestive and nerve health.

Ingredients

- 1/2 cup strawberries, fresh or frozen

- 1/2 cup blueberries, fresh or frozen

- 1/2 cup raspberries, fresh or frozen

- 1 cup spinach leaves

- 1/2 cup plain Greek yogurt

- 1/2 cup almond milk (or any milk of choice)

- Honey or maple syrup of 1 tablespoon (optional)

Mode of Preparation

1. Place all ingredients in a blender.

2. Blend until smooth and creamy, adding more milk if necessary to reach desired consistency.

3. Taste and adjust sweetness with honey or maple syrup if desired.

4. Pour into glasses and serve immediately.

Nutritional Information (per serving)

- Calories: 150 kcal

- Protein: 8g

- Fat: 2g

- Carbohydrates: 25g

- Fiber: 6g

- Sugar: 15g

Serving Size: 1 smoothie

Preparation Time: 5 minutes

2: Tropical Paradise

Health Benefits

- Pineapple is rich in bromelain, an enzyme with anti-inflammatory properties that can help reduce neuropathic symptoms.

- Mango provides vitamins and antioxidants that promote nerve health and reduce oxidative stress.

- Coconut milk is high in healthy fats and electrolytes, supporting nerve function and hydration.

Ingredients

- 1 cup frozen pineapple chunks

- 1/2 cup frozen mango chunks

- 1/2 ripe banana

- 1/2 cup coconut milk

- 1/2 cup plain Greek yogurt

- 1 tablespoon chia seeds

Mode of Preparation

1. Combine all ingredients in a blender.

2. Blend until smooth and creamy.

3. Taste and adjust sweetness by adding more banana if desired.

4. Pour into glasses and sprinkle with chia seeds before serving.

Nutritional Information (per serving)

- Calories: 200 kcal

- Protein: 8g

- Fat: 7g

- Carbohydrates: 30g

- Fiber: 6g

- Sugar: 20g

Serving Size: 1 smoothie

Preparation Time: 5 minutes

3: Green Powerhouse

Health Benefits

- Kale is rich in vitamins and antioxidants that support nerve health and reduce inflammation.

- Avocado provides healthy fats and vitamin E, which promote nerve function and reduce neuropathic symptoms.

- Almond butter adds protein and magnesium, supporting nerve health and reducing oxidative stress.

Ingredients

- 1 cup kale leaves, stems removed

- 1/2 ripe avocado

- 1/2 banana

- 1 tablespoon almond butter

- 1 cup almond milk (or any milk of choice)

- Honey or maple syrup of 1 tablespoon (optional)

Mode of Preparation

1. Place all ingredients in a blender.

2. Blend until smooth and creamy.

3. Taste and adjust sweetness with honey or maple syrup if desired.

4. Pour into glasses and serve immediately.

Nutritional Information (per serving)

- Calories: 250 kcal

- Protein: 8g

- Fat: 15g

- Carbohydrates: 25g

- Fiber: 7g

- Sugar: 15g

Serving Size: 1 smoothie

Preparation Time: 5 minutes

4: Banana-Oat Breakfast Smoothie

Health Benefits

- Bananas are high in potassium and vitamin B6, which support nerve function and reduce neuropathic symptoms.

- Oats provide fiber and complex carbohydrates that help regulate blood sugar levels and support nerve health.

- Almond milk is low in calories and contains vitamin E, which promotes nerve health and reduces oxidative stress.

Ingredients

- 1 ripe banana

- 1/4 cup rolled oats

- 1 tablespoon almond butter

- 1 cup almond milk (or any milk of choice)

- Honey or maple syrup of 1 teaspoon (optional)

- 1/2 teaspoon cinnamon

Mode of Preparation

1. Place all ingredients in a blender.

2. Blend until smooth and creamy.

3. Taste and adjust sweetness with honey or maple syrup if desired.

4. Pour into glasses and sprinkle with cinnamon before serving.

Nutritional Information (per serving)

- Calories: 250 kcal

- Protein: 6g

- Fat: 8g

- Carbohydrates: 40g

- Fiber: 6g

- Sugar: 15g

Serving Size: 1 smoothie

Preparation Time: 5 minutes

5: Chocolate Peanut Butter Protein Smoothie

Health Benefits

- Cocoa powder is rich in antioxidants and flavonoids that promote nerve health and reduce oxidative stress.

- Peanut butter provides protein, healthy fats, and vitamin E, supporting nerve function and reducing neuropathic symptoms.

- Greek yogurt adds protein and probiotics, supporting digestive and nerve health.

Ingredients

- 1 tablespoon cocoa powder

- 2 tablespoons peanut butter

- 1/2 cup plain Greek yogurt

- 1/2 banana

- 1 cup almond milk (or any milk of choice)

- Honey or maple syrup of 1 tablespoon (optional)

Mode of Preparation

1. Place all ingredients in a blender.

2. Blend until smooth and creamy.

3. Taste and adjust sweetness with honey or maple syrup if desired.

4. Pour into glasses and serve immediately.

Nutritional Information (per serving)

- Calories: 300 kcal

- Protein: 15g

- Fat: 15g

- Carbohydrates: 30g

- Fiber: 6g

- Sugar: 20g

Serving Size: 1 smoothie

Preparation Time: 5 minutes

6: Almond Berry Bliss

Health Benefits

- Almonds provide healthy fats, vitamin E, and magnesium, supporting nerve function and reducing neuropathic symptoms.

- Mixed berries are rich in antioxidants and vitamins that promote nerve health and reduce oxidative stress.

- Spinach adds folate and magnesium, supporting nerve function and reducing neuropathic symptoms.

Ingredients

- 1/4 cup almonds

- 1/2 cup mixed berries (strawberries, blueberries, raspberries)

- 1 cup spinach leaves

- 1/2 ripe banana

- 1 cup almond milk (or any milk of choice)

- Honey or maple syrup of 1 tablespoon (optional)

Mode of Preparation

1. In a blender, combine almonds, mixed berries, spinach leaves, ripe banana, almond milk, and honey or maple syrup (if using).

2. Blend until smooth and creamy.

3. Taste and adjust sweetness with additional honey or maple syrup if desired.

4. Pour into glasses and serve immediately.

Nutritional Information (per serving)

- Calories: 250 kcal

- Protein: 8g

- Fat: 12g

- Carbohydrates: 30g

- Fiber: 7g

- Sugar: 15g

Serving Size: 1 smoothie

Preparation Time: 5 minutes

7: Pineapple Coconut Delight

Health Benefits

- Pineapple contains bromelain, an enzyme with anti-inflammatory properties that can help reduce neuropathic symptoms.

- Coconut milk is high in healthy fats and electrolytes, supporting nerve function and hydration.

- Banana provides potassium and vitamin B6, which support nerve health and reduce neuropathic symptoms.

Ingredients

- 1 cup frozen pineapple chunks

- 1/2 ripe banana

- 1/4 cup coconut milk

- 1/4 cup plain Greek yogurt

- 1 tablespoon shredded coconut (optional)

- Honey or maple syrup of 1 tablespoon (optional)

Mode of Preparation

1. Combine frozen pineapple chunks, ripe banana, coconut milk, plain Greek yogurt, shredded coconut (if using), and honey or maple syrup (if using) in a blender.

2. Blend until smooth and creamy.

3. Taste and adjust sweetness with additional honey or maple syrup if desired.

4. Pour into glasses and serve immediately.

Nutritional Information (per serving)

- Calories: 200 kcal

- Protein: 6g

- Fat: 8g

- Carbohydrates: 30g

- Fiber: 4g

- Sugar: 20g

Serving Size: 1 smoothie

Preparation Time: 5 minutes

8: Mango Ginger Zinger

Health Benefits

- Mango is rich in vitamins and antioxidants that promote nerve health and reduce oxidative stress.

- Ginger has anti-inflammatory properties that can help reduce neuropathic symptoms.

- Greek yogurt provides protein and probiotics, supporting digestive and nerve health.

Ingredients

- 1 cup frozen mango chunks

- 1/2 inch piece of fresh ginger, peeled and grated

- 1/2 cup plain Greek yogurt

- 1/2 cup almond milk (or any milk of choice)

- Honey or maple syrup of 1 tablespoon (optional)

- Juice of 1/2 lime

Mode of Preparation

1. In a blender, combine frozen mango chunks, grated fresh ginger, plain Greek yogurt, almond milk, honey or maple syrup (if using), and lime juice.

2. Blend until smooth and creamy.

3. Taste and adjust sweetness with additional honey or maple syrup if desired.

4. Pour into glasses and serve immediately.

Nutritional Information (per serving)

- Calories: 200 kcal

- Protein: 8g

- Fat: 2g

- Carbohydrates: 35g

- Fiber: 4g

- Sugar: 25g

Serving Size: 1 smoothie

Preparation Time: 5 minutes

9: Green Tea Berry Booster

Health Benefits

- Green tea is rich in antioxidants and polyphenols that promote nerve health and reduce inflammation.

- Mixed berries provide vitamins and antioxidants that support nerve health and reduce oxidative stress.

- Greek yogurt adds protein and probiotics, supporting digestive and nerve health.

Ingredients

- 1/2 cup brewed green tea, chilled

- 1/2 cup mixed berries (strawberries, blueberries, raspberries)

- 1/2 cup plain Greek yogurt

- 1/2 ripe banana

- Honey or maple syrup of 1 tablespoon (optional)

- Ice cubes (optional)

Mode of Preparation

1. In a blender, combine chilled brewed green tea, mixed berries, plain Greek yogurt, ripe banana, and honey or maple syrup (if using).

2. Add ice cubes if desired for a colder smoothie.

3. Blend until smooth and creamy.

4. Taste and adjust sweetness with additional honey or maple syrup if desired.

5. Pour into glasses and serve immediately.

Nutritional Information (per serving)

- Calories: 150 kcal

- Protein: 8g

- Fat: 2g

- Carbohydrates: 30g

- Fiber: 5g

- Sugar: 20g

Serving Size: 1 smoothie

Preparation Time: 5 minutes

10: Chocolate Avocado Dream

Health Benefits

- Avocado provides healthy fats and vitamin E, which support nerve function and reduce neuropathic symptoms.

- Cocoa powder is rich in antioxidants and flavonoids that promote nerve health and reduce oxidative stress.

- Greek yogurt adds protein and probiotics, supporting digestive and nerve health.

Ingredients

- 1/2 ripe avocado

- 1 tablespoon cocoa powder

- 1 tablespoon honey or maple syrup

- 1/2 cup plain Greek yogurt

- 1/2 cup almond milk (or any milk of choice)

- Ice cubes (optional)

Mode of Preparation

1. In a blender, combine ripe avocado, cocoa powder, honey or maple syrup, plain Greek yogurt, and almond milk.

2. Add ice cubes if desired for a colder smoothie.

3. Blend until smooth and creamy.

4. Taste and adjust sweetness with additional honey or maple syrup if desired.

5. Pour into glasses and serve immediately.

Nutritional Information (per serving)

- Calories: 250 kcal

- Protein: 8g

- Fat: 12g

- Carbohydrates: 30g

- Fiber: 6g

- Sugar: 20g

Serving Size: 1 smoothie

Preparation Time: 5 minutes

NOTE

CHAPTER 6

Conclusion

This cookbook offers a comprehensive guide to creating delicious and nutritious meals tailored specifically for individuals managing peripheral neuropathy. By focusing on ingredients that support nerve health, reduce inflammation, and alleviate neuropathic symptoms, these recipes empower individuals to take control of their diet and overall well-being.

Throughout the cookbook, we've explored the importance of incorporating key nutrients such as vitamin B12, omega-3 fatty acids, antioxidants, and phytonutrients into daily meals to support nerve function and combat oxidative stress. From breakfast to dinner, snacks to smoothies, each recipe is thoughtfully crafted with the nutritional needs of peripheral neuropathy patients in mind.

By embracing a diet rich in whole foods, lean proteins, healthy fats, and fiber, individuals can optimize their nutritional intake while enjoying flavorful and satisfying meals. Whether it's starting the day with a nutrient-packed smoothie, savoring a nourishing bowl of soup for lunch, or indulging in a wholesome dinner, this cookbook provides a variety of options to suit every taste and preference.

Ultimately, by making mindful food choices and adopting healthy eating habits, individuals can enhance their quality of life and better manage the challenges associated with peripheral neuropathy. This cookbook serves as a valuable resource and companion on the journey to improved health and well-being, one delicious recipe at a time.

THANKS FOR READING

DAILY MEAL PLANNER

DAY/DATE: ______________________________

BREAKFAST

GROCERY LIST

LUNCH

DINNER

SNACKS

NOTES

DAILY MEAL PLANNER

DAY/DATE: _______________________________

BREAKFAST

GROCERY LIST

LUNCH

DINNER

SNACKS

NOTES

DAILY MEAL PLANNER

DAY/DATE: _______________________________

BREAKFAST

GROCERY LIST

LUNCH

DINNER

SNACKS

NOTES

DAILY MEAL PLANNER

DAY/DATE: _______________________________

BREAKFAST

GROCERY LIST

LUNCH

DINNER

SNACKS

NOTES

DAILY MEAL PLANNER

DAY/DATE: ______________________________

BREAKFAST

GROCERY LIST

LUNCH

DINNER

SNACKS

NOTES

DAILY MEAL PLANNER

DAY/DATE: _______________________________

BREAKFAST

GROCERY LIST

LUNCH

DINNER

SNACKS

NOTES

DAILY MEAL PLANNER

DAY/DATE: _______________________________

BREAKFAST

GROCERY LIST

LUNCH

DINNER

SNACKS

NOTES

DAILY MEAL PLANNER

DAY/DATE: _______________________________

BREAKFAST

LUNCH

DINNER

SNACKS

GROCERY LIST

NOTES

DAILY MEAL PLANNER

DAY/DATE: _______________________________

BREAKFAST

GROCERY LIST

LUNCH

DINNER

SNACKS

NOTES

DAILY MEAL PLANNER

DAY/DATE: ___________________________

BREAKFAST

GROCERY LIST

LUNCH

DINNER

SNACKS

NOTES

DAILY MEAL PLANNER

DAY/DATE: _______________________

BREAKFAST

LUNCH

DINNER

SNACKS

GROCERY LIST

NOTES

DAILY MEAL PLANNER

DAY/DATE: _______________________________

BREAKFAST

LUNCH

DINNER

GROCERY LIST

SNACKS

NOTES

DAILY MEAL PLANNER

DAY/DATE: _______________________

BREAKFAST

LUNCH

DINNER

SNACKS

GROCERY LIST

NOTES

DAILY MEAL PLANNER

DAY/DATE: _______________________________

BREAKFAST

GROCERY LIST

LUNCH

DINNER

SNACKS

NOTES

DAILY MEAL PLANNER

DAY/DATE: ______________________________

BREAKFAST

GROCERY LIST

LUNCH

DINNER

SNACKS

NOTES

DAILY MEAL PLANNER

DAY/DATE: _______________________________

BREAKFAST	GROCERY LIST

LUNCH

DINNER

SNACKS	NOTES

DAILY MEAL PLANNER

DAY/DATE: _______________________________

BREAKFAST

LUNCH

DINNER

SNACKS

GROCERY LIST

NOTES

DAILY MEAL PLANNER

DAY/DATE: _______________________________

BREAKFAST

LUNCH

DINNER

GROCERY LIST

SNACKS

NOTES

DAILY MEAL PLANNER

DAY/DATE: ______________________________

BREAKFAST

GROCERY LIST

LUNCH

DINNER

SNACKS

NOTES

DAILY MEAL PLANNER

DAY/DATE: _______________________________

BREAKFAST

GROCERY LIST

LUNCH

DINNER

SNACKS

NOTES

DAILY MEAL PLANNER

DAY/DATE: _______________________________

BREAKFAST

GROCERY LIST

LUNCH

DINNER

SNACKS

NOTES

DAILY MEAL PLANNER

DAY/DATE: _______________________________

BREAKFAST

GROCERY LIST

LUNCH

DINNER

SNACKS

NOTES

DAILY MEAL PLANNER

DAY/DATE: _______________________________

BREAKFAST

LUNCH

DINNER

SNACKS

GROCERY LIST

NOTES

DAILY MEAL PLANNER

DAY/DATE: _______________________________

BREAKFAST

GROCERY LIST

LUNCH

DINNER

SNACKS

NOTES

DAILY MEAL PLANNER

DAY/DATE: ___________________________

BREAKFAST

GROCERY LIST

LUNCH

DINNER

SNACKS

NOTES

DAILY MEAL PLANNER

DAY/DATE: _______________________________

BREAKFAST

LUNCH

DINNER

SNACKS

GROCERY LIST

NOTES

DAILY MEAL PLANNER

DAY/DATE: _______________________________

BREAKFAST

LUNCH

DINNER

SNACKS

GROCERY LIST

NOTES

DAILY MEAL PLANNER

DAY/DATE: _______________________

BREAKFAST

LUNCH

DINNER

GROCERY LIST

SNACKS

NOTES